ONE BODY

ONE BODY

Poems

———— ⚜ ————

MARGARET GIBSON

LOUISIANA STATE UNIVERSITY PRESS

BATON ROUGE

This publication is supported in part by an award from the National Endowment for the Arts.

NATIONAL
ENDOWMENT
FOR THE ARTS

Published by Louisiana State University Press
Copyright © 2007 by Margaret Gibson
All rights reserved
Manufactured in the United States of America
First printing
DESIGNER: Jenny Green
TYPEFACE: Requiem
PRINTER AND BINDER: Thomson-Shore, Inc

LIBRARY OF CONGRESS CATALOGING-IN-PUBLICATION DATA

Gibson, Margaret, 1944–
One body : poems / Margaret Gibson
p. cm.
ISBN-13: 978-0-8071-3239-5 (alk. paper)
ISBN-13: 978-0-8071-3240-1 (pbk. : alk. paper)
I. Title.
PS3557.I1916O54 2007
811′.54—dc22

2006031949

The author expresses grateful thanks to the editors of the following publications, in which the poems listed first appeared, sometimes in slightly different form: *American Poetry Journal*, "Air and Earth," "Spool of Red Thread" as "Elegy" (both 2004); *Arts and Letters*, "Respect" (2006); *Blackbird*, "East Window, Moon" (2006); *Chautauqua Literary Journal*, "Washing the Pitcher" (2004); *Connecticut Review*, "Elegy for My Father," "Still Life with Binoculars," "Transparent" (all 2006); *Gettysburg Review*, "The Waiting" as "Waiting I," "Meaning God, She Said *Light*" as "Waiting II" (both 2004); *Georgia Review*, "A Leaf of Basil," "Ashes," "Iris" ("Where are you now, old soul?") (all 2003); *Image*, "Poetry Is the Spirit of the Dead, Watching" (2006); *Inkwell*, "What Cannot Be Kissed Away," "Last Words," "Comfort," "Psalm" (all 2004); *Iowa Review*, "Cooking Supper While My Sister Dies," "Fuel," "Moment," "On Being Asked If the Anklet I'm Wearing Is an Old Charm Bracelet of Mine" (all 2006); *Kestrel*, "Dark Night I," "Dark Night II," "Dark Night III" (all 2007); *Shenandoah*, "Yonder" (2006); *Southern Poetry Review*, "My Mother's Girdle" (2003); *Southern Review*, "Lilies of the Valley" as "Elegy," "Iris" ("On its tall stalk, petals deep amethyst"), "The Gaze" (all 2006); *Spirituality and Health*, "Trying to Pray" (2006); *Worcester Review*, "In January, the Morning after the State of the Union Address, I Go Outside to Stand in Snowfall and Cold Air" (2004).

"One Body" appeared in *America Zen: A Gathering of Poets*, ed. Ray McNiece and Larry Smith (Huron: Bottom Dog Press, 2004).

"Ask Me Now," as "Icon," appeared in Part IV of *Icon and Evidence* (Baton Rouge: Louisiana State University Press, 2001). I reprint it in *One Body* for the fullness of understanding it brings to "Respect" and "Cooking Supper While My Sister Dies."

This book is for Isabelle, Rachel, and Anneka.

What is it when the wind is blowing
and the trees are bare?
The golden wind, revealed.

CONTENTS

I

WASHING THE PITCHER

The long day after she died,
before the unmerciful
questions returned,
I found on a low shelf
tucked into the dark
the small Delft pitcher,
around it and inside it
sleek black flecks
not unlike coarsely milled
black pepper, the tell-tale
evidence of mice.
On every vase or pitcher
in that cupboard, on every plate
a thick blur of dust.
I might have washed
all, or any one of them,
but it was this one, blue
and white, I wanted
and with a certainty that felt
unreasonable and right.
And so I stood at the sink
where each evening she'd stood
washing the supper potatoes
rinsing lettuce or fruit
ignoring her tiredness,
making her lists, perhaps
repeating a prayer, her gaze
on the rain gauge outside
in the grass or on the garden's
broken gate
festooned with late summer
sweet peas, pink and white.
Rinsed to a shine, the pitcher,
set down on the window sill,
brimmed with light—

so that when I turned back
to the room, it was not
to the chaos of sorting and boxing,
setting to rest her things,
each one a mute testament
to a life that once
had silence and value and voice.
No. When I turned, I was
like a woman in a painting
by Vermeer, my cap starched
white, the copper plates
polished, sunlight spilling
from the open casement
into the room, into the next room,
and the next. When I turned,
the table was set for breakfast,
east light on the round oak table,
light on the aluminum toaster,
on the glasses of juice. There were
cloth napkins in their wooden rings,
blue mats, yellow plates and cups,
a single jonquil in the bud vase
on the lazy Susan, and a hand—
Jean's hand—reaching
to turn nearer
the small blue and white pitcher,
rinsed and revealed, just as it is
in the moment full of light.

THE WAITING

Back-lit by the river light that filled her window
        in the nursing wing,
                she'd balance on
her only leg: then
a sudden pivot

as we'd help her slowly over into her afternoon
        chair. When the nurses
                soaked and changed the bandages
on her foot, flesh
lifted away,

her toes gone black. And to deflect
        what I felt
                into what I could
bear to think, I'd think
of the great egret

at the margin of our pond, how it lifts
        and holds close to its body
                one black stilt,
keeping its delicate
balance,

steadily looking into its own
        reflection: an impersonal
                hunger in its belly,
fierce precision
in its eye—

it doesn't think *I'm alone*. It doesn't
        think *I'm alone*
                in a body that can't
love me.

MEANING GOD, SHE SAID *LIGHT*

In just light, David limbed the white pines
  that threatened her house.
    In just light, I weeded her garden
  watching one by one
the buds of the Stargazer

swell and its central stalk stoop over the garden's
  stone wall, then bloom:
    the weight of pain married to
  the odor of the implicit
body: body

that longs to be body *and* light: body that belongs
  to river light and ruin.
    Sweet ruin, tell me
  what shall we pray for?
So that with suppleness of will we may

bend to this lavish scattering.

A LEAF OF BASIL

I never understood the words
Take, eat . . . until
Joan brought to the hospital
a sprig of basil, and Jean,
who hadn't eaten
more than a daily mouthful,
keeping her eyes closed,
put her hand on Joan's
and drew the basil close.
Breathed it in, smiled,
paused—then, guiding the basil
into her mouth, ate.
Ate all of Greece,
Corfu especially, and Crete.
Ate goat cheese and a crust
of bread, the dust
of ruins and wild thyme.
Kissed her dead husband's
living mouth, wrapped
around her body
a wide shawl
from Oaxaca's market.
Wrote in her journal.
Folded clothing
for those made homeless
by war, said
something in Italian,
in Spanish, in German.
Said *light*. Remembered
merriment and evening wine.
Uncorked new bottles
she'd made from dandelions
gathered in fields
thick with sun. Walked
outside at night to watch

the slow, sudden comet
arc between the cedars.
Made her way to the garden
to harvest beans.
Sat quietly with friends.
Set the table, mended socks,
tended whatever needed
tending—for of such
is the kingdom of heaven.
And wasn't it heaven
and earth entire
she swallowed? One leaf.
Absolute and momentary.
Leaf of final emptiness
and harvest,
leaf of open windows
and self-watchful passion.
Leaf of Antares, Arcturus,
lamplight and fountain.
One leaf, she took.
One leaf, she breathed.
One leaf, she *was* . . .

WHAT CANNOT BE KISSED AWAY

What am I going to do now? she wrote
in her journal.

Counting her losses, she confessed
just once

she was angry with God.
                    Who else? she said.

To understand her going blind, I close my eyes.

To sense what it would be like
both legs gone

I tuck my own legs under me
and sit
           facing the dark.

It's the best I can do.

Trying to imagine with my body
what was come here to do

having finished.

LAST WORDS

I wanted her words to make sense.

I wanted to think her suffering
made each word count.

On Sunday, she asked to dictate a letter.

To David Cornfield:
> *Dear David,*
How much is seven cornfields?
At how much? And how much
per cornfield? I am very strict.

She was propped up by pillows,
as short in the bed as a child,
each remaining thigh
swaddled, plump as a loaf.

"No, no pain," she lied.

"I don't know," she said. "I don't know."

"Someone must come."

COMFORT

I wade into the pond and reach down
for the roots of the pond lilies,
roots that reef and tangle into the mud.
Tugging. Falling back from the force
of their letting go. Reaching into
the snarled and braided tenements,
bumped now and again by the fish
that feed on these moorings.

Putting my face under, coiling the long
whips of stems with their flat pads and buds,
heaving them to the shore.
Still angry that she must suffer so.
Wishing the root of her pain weren't
so hidden, so human.
Wishing God were not inside me.

A green frog stretches out on a lily pad,
watchful. I want to assure it
I won't pull up all the lilies in my fury.
The root of *comfort,* and the motive,
I remind myself, is strength, not ease.
Out of the depths I cry to Thee,
O God . . . what's the rest of it?

I tug up from the murk and silt
a raft of root, long stems, a few blossoms
floating after, like the wake of an ecstasy
or a flush of pain, my hands now
stained purple by the lilies, black by the mud.
The same hands that fumbled through
her Psalter and couldn't find the one
she wanted, couldn't find my way.

Whither shall I go from Thy Spirit?
If I take the wings of the morning and dwell
in the uttermost parts of the sea, even there . . .

I read her that instead.

PSALM

As I read the psalm, she lifted from the bed
        both her arms: briefly, not far:
            then let them fall
                alongside her, as if to say
I have taken the blow, and it is good.

Shall I keep reading? I asked. She nodded.
        The vein in her neck beat fast,

her eyes stayed shut. She never said
        my name, nor did it matter
            who I was: *that* was
                her gift, her teaching.
She was laying herself aside—

so I read until the sound of my voice became
        her breathing, her breathing

the wind that lulls and falls off, sundering
        sentence and skein, unraveling
            back to the Source
                O resourceful Maker,
innermost: beyond our names.

DARK NIGHT I

Her breathing changed—

as when a hearth fire
flickers, nearly out

and one takes a bellows
and pumps it,

a rapid chuffing.

Then a pause,
to see if the fire takes.

All night her breathing
was like this.

Perhaps the spent body's way
of asking itself,

Are you sure? Are you sure?

DARK NIGHT II

Presence
cannot be verified

by breath alone.

Nor can it be inhaled
like the smell of the fresh peach

I brought to tempt her back into her life.

Within reach

all night it ripened.

DARK NIGHT III

When her eyes fluttered open
    it was night. When they closed again, night.

Night when her gaze met mine, her eyes fully open.

Dark night and open when I cried out
    and put my head on her shoulder. Night

when I closed her eyes and continued to sit with her.
    Dark night, dark night.

In which everything, and nothing, is—whether I can see it
    or not.

IRIS

Where are you now, old soul?

I ask, just here by your door stone
                transplanting iris,
                        the blue flags
        whose corms twist and knot into mats
                so thick, I must

change into the one who strove with the nameless
                angel at Peniel,
                        strove and prevailed.
        Without knowing it, face to face
                with God.

But I'm not made for this work, I think.
                Even your husband
                        turned the air blue
        with his efforts to wrest these iris
                out of the earth.

Stones rest solidly in themselves.
                These iris, these rainbows
                        with roots, must have
        made a pact with stones, a covenant.
        Steadfast, hold fast.

On your last day, I swallowed hard and said
                you were loved—by so many
                        loved. But if
        your spirit needs to go, I said,
                let it go.

Now I can't believe you're not here.
                Feel me tugging, tugging—
                        as if these iris,

this house, autumn sun, my own
sweat might just give

back, hard-won and humble, your presence.
In the smell of the dirt,
in the low call of the owl,
you: you knelt here, tugged iris,
turned your head

to glimpse sun-flash and wing-shadow
sweeping over the grass,
with no need to say,
I will not let you go until you bless me—
already blessed.

ASHES

It rained. Further inland
the road was a black mirror that held
in a wet shimmer gold maples
and the boughs of evergreens
bent with early snow. Between
the White Mountains and the distant
ridges of the Green, the valley lifted,
floating in the mists. *All the way
to heaven is heaven,* I thought,
as if we carried your ashes
into a Chinese painting. As if
Charles Chu had painted the day
and hung it in panels, the world
of earth and sky your living room.

In the graveyard at North Sebago,
near the lake, we dug you in,
lifting a flap of sod.
Work to simplify the heart, you
advised. We dug, then took
the two white boxes, your ashes
and his, and put them side by side.
Then stood silent. How small
they were, the boxes,
rimmed by a frame of wet earth
that showed the strict, raw marks
of the shovel. The rain fell
steadily, the rim contracted,
as if it were the iris of an eye
or a telescope. All I could see
were those two white forms,
which widened
to include the whole
mind and body of the world.

So that, after we rolled the sod
back over and sealed it,
I knew there were, beneath my feet,
mountains and a lake, clouds,
and the moon clear and still
behind the mist and daylight,
through which two figures emerged,
an old hoe tilted at rest on his shoulder,
in her hand a basket—light green
to heighten the effect of the mountains,
the weave of the basket
rendered in strokes like the veins
of a lotus leaf, like ax cuts, raveled rope.

II

NEWSPAPER PHOTOGRAPH

Beneath a band of broken cloud-light, in silhouette against the morning sky
    a line of women climbs the stone embankment,

a rising line of women, single file, each with a basket balanced on her head—
    migrant women, the caption says,

carrying stones in a quarry in India.

They are Bangladeshi—but to my distanced eye they could be figures in a frieze
    on a temple architrave,

or a repeating detail in black slip on a potsherd fired before the fifth century,

women with bowls or vessels on their heads, women with wide, shallow baskets—
    their necks taut and strong, their heads at a tilt

through the centuries carrying oil, carrying wine, carrying the harvest grains
    a civilization depends on.

But these are women in a stone quarry, and the morning mist, I realize,

isn't mist at all, but a dust that soils their saris, burns their eyes, silts
    into their ears—they eat dust with each breath

as they climb the rise to spill an offering of stones into the machine at the crest,
    then turn back on the sloped path

to the stone heap, whose rim-line resembles Mount Meru, to refill their baskets.
    And now I see how their coming and going

makes a wheel: a wheel of life and death: a mandala that would interest
    you, Gautam Mukerjee,

wry economist and lover of justice, who once as a child on pilgrimage
    in the mountains above the Ganges

looked steeply up and saw against the brilliant sky a white bird, its wings

outspread as it spiraled into a blaze of light—*a sign,* you said, sent
    by the holy man toward whom your journey tended,

the silent voice of the gods made visible—as all such images are: at the least
    a caution: a leading: a prayer:

God, make me see.

THE GAZE

Why, in the middle of the night, in the sleepless interval it takes
the horned moon to pass the peak of the south cedar, sliding west,
do I remember, years ago, that young man who from his bike downhill

reached out and touched one of my breasts as he sped by?
I was walking, en route to the college, mulling over the stanzaic pattern
of Keats's *Ode to a Grecian Urn* when I saw him.

He had already sped by me once, on the tarmac, dressed like
a yellow-jacket in a helmet—so why was he here again, coming straight
toward me, so soon, this time on the sidewalk I walked on?

There were no cars on the road that passed over the turnpike.
The ground to my left fell steeply away beyond the guard rail
into an alcove of wasteland. Ironweed, broken bottles, wire.

No way to avoid him, I held his gaze. I let him know I saw him, too—
although now I recall how sexless was the squeeze
he gave my breast. Not tentative—no, no. It was deliberate,

if also dispassionate. He might have been trying a goat's teat
before milking it. Puckish, too. *I could do more, but I won't,*
said his hand, his mouth ruled in a straight line of shutness.

All the way downhill, from the moment I understood he was
coming for me, his eyes—blue, cold, hard as he was
on the saddle seat of his chrome and steel speed bike—

held mine, screwdriver to screw. I looked into the gaze of
a loathing so transparent I understood that the dark spirits of rape,
ethnic cleansing, interrogation, and self-hatred

were distilled there in a mockery of the lover's gaze—
so that after he poked me, squeezed, and let me live
I thought in numb denial, *So I have been bruised by a god.*

A rueful, even a silly, thought. Better that, than to have turned the moment from its understated terror, taking his gaze inward, ashamed that I wore my summer blouse too tight.

IN JANUARY, THE MORNING AFTER THE STATE OF THE UNION ADDRESS, I GO OUTSIDE TO STAND IN SNOWFALL AND COLD AIR

just to breathe, I tell myself
as if I
      or anyone
might start over, the public slate
wiped clean. No greed, no war,
no fear of war declared by others
in my name. The shame of it.

Then, loud from leafless thickets
now plumed white with camouflage
lifts the song of a winter wren,
a swirl of notes that enters the scant
descending descant of the snow—
just what is: no more.
                  Do they think
we are fools? I mutter into
my scarf as I kick a stone
I let stand for the war they have
so carefully provoked—that is,
the wars.
      How seldom
we see ourselves as we are,
naked as birth-cry.
It's hard to see, to know,
to speak clearly
breathing in the invisible ash
that is always here. We call it
confetti, smoke screen, snow—
as the ash blows in from
Iraq, from Chile and Nam Phen,
from My Lai, Alamogordo,
Washington, and Watts.

Nothing's now what it seems—
this snow and wind the mindless
sweep of consent to war;
the song of the winter wren the cry
of a child in Baghdad. Unless
in a change of heart and mind
somehow we change
the stone that stands for war
to a single, life-giving syllable—*No.*

FUEL

I am, said the voice in the oil spill of rainbow radiance,
the angel of El, from the deserts and gulfs of El.

I looked for a face, flesh and blood I might hold
accountable, a name. It saw right through me. *Uriel,*

Eliel, Emmanuel, Fuel, said the angel. *Fuel?* I replied,
and a human form stood before me, a merchant

who turned to measuring my life as if I were cloth,
judging length and price by the distance between his elbow

and the tip of his middle finger. The arm wore camouflage
the shade of sand and bone. *You do what suits me,*

Fuel smiled. He tossed the dead man's arm aside. *Grenade,*
he said. Arched his eyebrows, shrugged.

MOMENT

Just now, as I'm listening to the rain plink off the rim of the down-spout,
    she is walking toward the embassy,

the explosives hidden beneath her clothing, swaddled against her belly,
    warmed by her heat.

As I riffle through pages and pages of poems in Machado's *Times Alone*
    in search of the golden wind

that quickens words like *jasmine, lemon,* in Tuzla a young girl watches
    a man stumble to his knees

at the edge of a field, his hands tied behind him, and already she hears
    the clink of the shovel

that will uncover his bones, and those of the others, two winters and one
    harvest hence.

Listening and muttering, riffling and watching, I look up, startled to hear
    soaking into the stones at the edge

of the woods, *Cocoon! Cocoon!* the call of a dove, so murmurous and clear
    I could follow it gladly

into silence and green shade. *Not now,* I tell myself. *Not now.* Ask first
    what it is such silence mystifies.

Who it implicates, who protects. What it refuses, what construes.

RESPECT

I

How strange they were, how fearsome, with their lidless
    yellow eyes, the fierce and accurate
bobbing of their necks, the flounce of burnished tail feathers,
    the way each yellow foot
lifted itself, flexed its nubbly toes, spread them out and set
    them down in slow motion
while the fury of their bobbing necks kept up a rapt staccato
    near my bare toes.
In the midst of them stood Edwin, no shirt, baggy overalls,
    holding a hen by
the ankle part, her feet sticking out the back of a hand big as
    a baseball mitt.
Sun flashed off the head of the hatchet that hung in the rung
    of his overalls. With his back
turned, he was whistling! Whistling, he didn't have to see us,
    Betsy and me—why should he
have to deal with Miss Doyle's city girls? The chicken,
    now a flapping squawk of feathers,
grew quiet, stilled perhaps by Edwin's gait, a lumbering
    that rolled over the earth
and knew it round, a stolid rocking that took him over
    to the wide stump of wood.
I let myself be drawn there, coming near with my body,
    moving away in my mind.
In a motion so swift it was seamless, like light, down came
    naked arm, steel edge,
and the weight of Edwin's determination to give Aunt T
    what she'd asked for,
Sunday dinner. All this met in the hen's neck, which I knew
    from sucking one in Brunswick stew
was an interlocked lace of bones. Soundlessly, over
    into the wood dust

went the hen's head, the eye yellow with a jet black center,
  the beak hard and bright.
I held my breath, my sister let out an explosion of giggles,
  pointing—for there in the dust,
released from Edwin's grasp, the chicken's body, headless,
  ran in swooping arcs about the wood yard,
looking for its head. "Do another one!" my sister demanded,
  delighted with the dancing dead hen.
"Miss T want two more hens for company Sunday," Edwin said.
  He wouldn't let us think
he'd kill another one because two white girls from the city,
  who didn't know what they were
looking at, the difference between life and death, had asked him.

II

Marie, my mother used to say, had white blood—that's why her skin
  was coffee with milk.
Edwin's, she said, was coffee without sugar or milk, and that's why
  he wanted nothing to do with
any of us, why he stayed outside when Marie plucked the hens
  in a bucket of water
hot as her hands could stand. I thought the palms of her hands
  were pink because
they'd faded in the scald of hot water. Thought again—no, were
  that so, her hands would be entirely pink.
Edwin's hands were light and dark, also the soles of his feet.
  Some things made no sense, and one of them
was color. Head down, hunched over, Marie held the bucket
  steady between her knees.
In hot water the red feathers turned dark brown, the yellow feet
  turned yellower.
Once they were cooked, Marie would take them and suck them—
  she said they were sweet.
I never asked Marie for a suck. Nor did she offer it. "The feet
  is mine," she said,

and she could have them, sticking up like broken witches', umbrellas,
    evil angles with curved
spurs. Sweat kerneled on Marie's forehead, slid down her neck
    into her dress where it darkened
the seams around her shoulders. She grunted softly as she yanked,
    then looked up.
"Law, child, you gonna faint? Run along now, run along."

III

And I did, I ran. It would take years before I'd see face to face
    on a city sidewalk
during the march in Memphis a black man with a sign hung round
    his neck, words
so simple and dignified and true, they stunned me. *I am a man.*
    Years more
before that city black man blurred, and I saw Edwin there
    and wondered hard
who he had been, and went back to Amelia, driving the curved
    country roads
until I recognized the red dirt lane that led to their small cabin
    with the well out back.
Marie lived there, but I'd come too late—Edwin, she said,
    had gone home to God;
her son Junior, home from a war with one arm and an empty
    sleeve pinned to his shirt,
lived up north near Bridgeport. She'd worked for the Harvies,
    one family or another of them,
all her life, she laughed, voice high and shrill, eyes bright.
    "Your sister," she asked, "she still fat?"
I wasn't ready to talk about my sister, still stung by Marie's reply
    when I said I'd come
in my mother's place. "No'm," she'd cried. "Ain't nobody takes
    Miss Doyle's place, nobody."
My face turned red as a beet in her garden—because hadn't I
    wanted to be the ambassador of better things?

Hadn't I wanted to supplant my mother, who'd still talk to me
    like this: "I've changed, you know.
I went to Willemina's funeral, afterwards right to her house.
    It was as clean as a white person's!"

IV

What Marie and I might have been to each other, had I come
    without wanting from her
something I couldn't yet give myself, I'll never know.
    I couldn't name it, then.
I sat on the sofa and showed her pictures of my family. I asked
    questions until she laughed,
"You one of them radicals?" She wiped her eyes, told me how
    back then,
when my mother first came to board with Miss T and teach
    in the two-room schoolhouse,
no one had money, not even the white folks. "I'd iron
    for the Garlands,
cook at the wood stove for Miss T, chop wood with Edwin
    at the sawmill.
It was *that way.*" Her voice settled on the words, and she
    didn't say anything for a while.
Then, as a quickening wind turns leaves on their backsides
    before a storm, she started up again—
Miss Mason, now there was a piece of work, didn't I remember
    Miss Mason? Tiny woman,
ate like a bird, pillar of the church? fine family? Well.
    On a day hot as fire, she said,
there on her big porch was Miss Mason, calling *Oh Marie,*
    you there, Marie!
"I stopped, put my milk pail in the shade. Mrs. Garland
    had give me some fresh
milk I had to get home, and here's Miss Mason, daughter
    of a judge, asking me

to clean fireplaces." As she must have done then, she
    paused. Asked how much
Miss Mason would give her. "*Fifty cents,*" she replied,
    her voice like velvet.
"When I finished, all four fireplaces clean as spit,
    she come over to me,
pretty as you please, and cool—she'd been on the porch
    in a good breeze—says,
Mercy me, Marie, look here. Her hand held out two coins.
    I looked in my purse, sure I had
two quarters, and here I find one quarter and this dime."
    It was the way
she said it. Said it so Marie would see she was smarter than
    any colored could hope to be.
Miss Mason's words in Marie's mouth—I could
    taste them.
And Marie? She had milk to get home. She couldn't say,
    "It's not enough, you gave
your word, could you pay me later?" One word, that's all
    it would take, one word, *uppity,*
and there she'd be, down on her luck, down on her knees
    clean 'cross the county.
"We were both polite," Marie said. "Polite, and
    slicker than the courthouse floor."
She paused. "Think about it. Both of us,
    so polite."

V

As a child, I thought I knew Marie. I knew her close smell,
    a cross between starch and lavender.
She let me swat flies when they got too bad in the kitchen,
    she let me pat the biscuits
onto the tin pans. She held me in her arms one afternoon
    when I came running in

so angry with my sister I could only blurt out, "I hate her,
    I hate her."
I can't remember now what my sister did to hurt me.
    I was keeping an unspoken
list of her sins, her stupidities—they were my secrets.
    They were evidence
I could use to prove we were different. I could
    turn my back and walk away
justified, unharmed, unafraid. It didn't matter
    we were sisters—we were
different, I told Marie. We had nothing in common,
    I hated her.
What Marie murmured to me, I took as comfort.
    Oh, Honey, she said
back then in the summer kitchen's heat. *Oh, Honey.*

ONE BODY

I am born in a field
of cornflowers and ripe wheat
wind in the black gum trees
late afternoon before the storm
and the men are cutting the field
working the mower in circles
coming in and in
toward the center of the field
where I crouch down
with the rabbits, with the quail
driven into this space by the clackety mower
because I want to see
how the body goes still
how the mind, how the lens of the eye
magnifies to an emptiness
so deep, so flared wide
there is everywhere field and the Source
of field, and only
a quiver of the nose
or the flick of a top-knot feather, a ripple
so faint I may have imagined it, says
yes, says *no*
to the nearing rustle in the last stand of wheat—
and now it's quiet, too quiet
a soft trample
a click, the cocking sound, a swish
as the men steal in to take
what they want
they are clever, they are hungry
and because this one body is
my birthplace
my birthright, my only homeplace
my nest and burrow and bower
I understand
my mother is wheat, my father is wind

and I rise in a tall gust
                of rage and compassion
I rise up from the mown and edible
            debris of the world
                    wrapped in a bright
net of pollen and stars, my thighs
            twin towers of lightning
                and my voice
I am a storm of voices, snipe and wolf
            snow goose, dolphin, quail, and lark—
                Stop this. Stop it now
I say to the men, who stalk closer
            keen on the kill, late light
                on the steel of their rifles
and they are my brothers—they are my brothers
            and I love them, too
                Look into my eyes
I tell them. *See for yourself the one shining field*
        Look into my eyes
                before you shoot

LILIES OF THE VALLEY

omes the nor'easter, with its churn of cold Atlantic air, the rough spit of it flung
    against clapboard and cedar shingles, a baffling whine at the windows,
buffeting in the maples that bend and bow over the pond ruched white by downpour,
    and look, tiny wells in the fine mesh of the screen door, which shudders,
nd none of it, none of it dims the insistent steadiness of scent in those
    slender bell flowers, inconspicuous at best, obscured
the thrash of rain, how they tremble, each one beneath an alcove of green leaf
    so like the mandorla behind a Bodhisattva—and no bells
ngled, neither raw soliloquy nor rant nor solicitous inquiry (our forms of grief),
    theirs only a steady dumbstruck essence, sweet, Lord, so sweet
passes understanding year by year as they return unabated, generous (like my father,
    who planted them), rising each season from their underworld of mud
nd stone and root, so fluent their beatitude I nearly understand how the meek
    can inherit the earth.

ELEGY FOR MY FATHER

Gifts

The Monday before he died,
he put on the new glasses
I'd sent at his request
and slipped onto his wrist
the new watch with the white hands
and blue face. For the time being
he was time being my father
as the watch on his wrist
counted out the four last days
he'd have in his body on earth.
When the pain blazed in his chest,
I want to believe he saw
only light as he melted into it.
You know where your father's
life is now? my friend asked
and gave me without a pause
these words, *It's in you.*

Word over All, Beautiful as the Sky

I'd asked to see him before he was
made up and clothed in the suit
I brought—labeled in his own
hand, *best suit, red stripe,*
a charcoal gray with an artery
of red in the weave.
And so I opened the door and found
him in the formal room,
before the folds of a pleated curtain,
on a table, two white sheets
softly folded back, so that just
his collarbone, neck, and head
met air. He was whiter than
the white cloth, colder
than my hands, which shook.
I touched first his hair, clean
and soft; both my hands
held his cheeks. I smoothed
his eyebrows, touched
his hands, the hard
bones of his knuckles severe,
unrelenting. I kissed him.
And whispered in his ear
words I knew were for my benefit.
If his spirit lingered in the room,
if he saw me tend the husk
he'd threshed from, he learned
nothing new. He knew, thank God,
I loved him. I don't know
how long I stayed there.
Somewhere the sky was clearing.
Night sky and sun sky
turning one into the other,
the slow debris of stars, of dust
and pollen, turning. And

I learned this. His body,
that coffin of snow,
was also cloud and rain light—
I would have to let him go.

Body of Light

My friend Jane has seen spirits—beneficent, fierce—and painted them,
storm-lit, eclipse-lit, dawn-lit
breath by breath, each breath drawn up from the depths
of an under-color unmistakably glowing,
as mutable as sky.

The horizon, how it shifts, washed by light.

On white paper, ruled with blue horizontal lines
and a single vertical to bound me,
                                now I write *father.*

In water, in fire, in air I write it—remembering
the particular, flushed, indigenous
earth smell of his skin.

Listening to Elgar's Sospiri

It's in the bass notes, slow as a fading
heartbeat. The resignation of it.
The restitution. It's how
quietly the music swells
and spreads, unrolling as a wave
momentarily certain on the shore,
assuring me: *he was ready.*
I had wanted to be with him—
he chose what we could bear.
Don't ask how I know. Perhaps
I don't know.
             But tonight
when David asked if I wanted a fire,
the spring night cold, and I said *yes,*
I was thinking of my father's ardent
spirit. I wanted that.
And when the fire failed
to catch and keep—too little
kindling and the oak log
thick—we were too weary
to fuss with it. An hour passed.
We read, had supper—
then of its own accord the fire blazed.
Sospiri, it flared and, for a moment,
I saw the fire inside the fire.
Call it what you will, the radiance
in the room had presence—*his.*

MY MOTHER'S GIRDLE

My mother isn't dead,
but I'm disposing of her things, unpacking
                two dressers, a closet
                    a pine chest
        weeding out old Christmas cards
and doctor's appointments, saved napkins and the
            little containers of jam
                she's taken
        from restaurants, afraid
she'll never have enough, never enough
                and wanting a "sweet touch"
                    at the close of a bitter day.
        As she's grown older,
she's fit herself into smaller and smaller rooms,
                moving from the only
                    house I can remember
        from my childhood
into retirement's doll house, then to a large room
                and assisted independence
                    where she made her bed
            throne and parliament—
now to a shared double in the nursing wing,
                for which I am saving
                    one dresser, a night stand
        an armchair, family pictures
a handkerchief angel, and the little stuffed lamb
                she puts under her pillow,
                    away from those who
            come in the night
to take things: her valuables, the predicates
                of her sentences, the names of those
                    who roam too quietly
        about the many mansions
of her Father's house. I unpack the starched
                linens she never used,

the blouses I sent her,
never worn and folded in with
pajamas I wore as a teenager, and a swimsuit.
Three Bibles, the prayers
she scribbled on the envelopes
of unopened bills and advertisements.
A tea towel I made in art class, fifth grade, with unevenly
blue ink-block prints of a sailboat
sailing off, sailing away.
No love letters, only
the aqua dress she wore to my wedding, and a fan from
the church in Amelia
where she married my father.
Ten pairs of white gloves,
a box of calling cards faded yellow, an old girdle—
the sateen of its belly-guard frayed
but still shining,
the upper border of elastic
bowed and rippled by the pressure of her upright flesh.
I hold it up, smooth it out,
then lock the door of the room
and lift my skirt
tugging it on, remembering how audibly she sighed
herself out of her Sunday's best,
the pent-up flesh inside the girdle
gratefully released
as she lowered the side zipper, bending over to unlatch
her nylons from the little tabs,
letting them fall to her ankles
then off with the high heels,
a tug to the girdle, down it went, hips to thighs
unburdened then wholly free
as the flesh that had been
hidden away met the flesh that had
gathered into rolls and bulged between the girdle
and her heavy bra—
it all came down,

melting down—as finally
now come my tears for this woman who tried
                    with her lists and commandments
                    and prayers
          to make herself good enough,
and the rest of us, shaping the lives that had
                    sprung from the depths of her,
                              fitting us into the fictions
          she told herself for comfort,
passing off the frayed story of her life
                    for life itself.
                         Who she wasn't,
          who she was—
do I know? I pull in my breath and my stomach,
                    turning sideways to the mirror.
                    Here is the belly
          that never had children,
a belly flatly swaddled in innocent sateen, stubbornly
                    empty with longing.
                         Oh, but I have rebelled
          enough. Right or wrong, I can love
her now—as only I can, as only I am—holding back just this,
          my childish fear
                    of her unsatisfied
heart, still so stubbornly holding on.

YONDER

Summer nights, I still smell the honeysuckle at the edge of her voice
    when she called me to listen to the bobwhites

across the field, their call and response a way to measure the interval
    between dusk and white blaze as the moon,

our distaff and shadow-bearing source of profusion, rose. Wild roses
    she called *God's grace.*

Ohh, she says now, drawing out the vowel, making do. Her words,
    like petals, have slipped by hank or handful

loose, and fallen in a clump at the foot of the last nodding peony.
    How I loved to hear her say *Chula, Coverly,*

place names I might now graft to a new brood of roses, or chant,
    giving weight to the nameless name of God.

Tonight the night is solstice bright, the moon close to brimming.
    How long does *long ago* last?

Bred in the bone, this ache to hold her. This hunger to know
    the child she has irrevocably become,

drawn so far inside herself I can't touch the hem of her cotton nightdress
    as she rises out of her body

and rambles beyond the spreading fields of wheat and stars, back
    through the orchard of pear trees, across the wild meadow,

slowly, oh so slowly, going home.

ASK ME NOW

I

To raise her spirits
someone has painted her toenails
with a lacquer clear as
the white of an egg but with flecks of glitter added in
to flash like mica,
like quartz in stone.
I have come a long way,
if the common measure of love
is loss, to rub her legs and her callused feet
with a lotion rich in lavender,
remembering how our mother
used to stand at the margin of our room, the door
narrowed open,
and sing into the dark where we lay unready for sleep,
an arbor of phosphorescent stars
pasted to the ceiling.
I don't know if the body believes the words
we offer it, or if it listens
only to the motive below the motive, octaves down—
but I still see her, about to withdraw,
and the stroke of light
that crossed the coverlet as her alto
patience and intimate
refrain lilted over us, like a hand stroking back
damp hair from a feverish forehead.
Side by side
in our twin beds, alone in the dark,
our small bodies
already ripening to the sweet danger within us—
to hear our mother sing to us
at the verge of limitless
night, the song offered up from the deep
harbor of her body,

must have gathered us, continued and carried us at rest
into the flushed, ready morning.
Ask me now
if I believe in resurrection, body and mind—
I'd have to hum
what little I remember of the song that carried us
all through the night that was
deeper than we could know.
"I've named my left arm Lazarus," she confides,
and I nod,
letting my hands, wiser than I am, work the song
measure by measure into the muscles
of her left arm and leg.
"I see you," she says, turning her body slowly
toward the side of herself
she neglects, finding me there. *I see you*—said
without surprise or particular
emphasis, as if I hadn't,
all these years, forgetting to remember her,
scorned and disregarded
part of my own heart. When finally I say, "See you
in the morning," she answers quickly,
"I'll be right here."

II

Alone in my own dark room,
I lift my head from hands so wet
with tears they smell like rain
in a field of lavender. Afraid for her life, abandoned and to come,
I flip open my journal
and I see the words,
Do not fear. Only believe,
and she shall be well. Only believe.

Credo, it means give your heart, give it scorned and abandoned
worthy and not worth much,
give it finally, freely.
What seems so far from you, I read,
is most your own.
I take the words into my body. Take them, sister,
into yours. They are light.
Or let me rub them lightly
on your skin, oil of lavender,
oil of rosemary and rue.
Alone in the body's dark nights, in its gardens and hovels,
in its rivers and mountains and many rooms,
together we lie down.

COOKING SUPPER WHILE MY SISTER DIES

She takes her last meal of sugar water and oblivion,
the needle keen as a knife, a double-edged bridge

she must cross into the Unsayable. *Wait,* I say, *wait*—
but she will not, nor can I go with her, delay

in each grain of rice, exile in the onions I chop so fine
I am word blind, my face wet with the rain

that was her grief, and mine, that we did not love
each other long enough. Black olives, then zucchini

diced, swept into a pan from the wooden board,
a heave offering to the wine-dark sea.

And I must . . . I can only . . . I am left with . . .
this tomato, sun-ripened and taut, tinged green

at the pock where it let go of the vine. Into hinged
wedges I cut it slowly. Slowly. Wanting

her to be like a flower that opens into a summer night
of stars, breath by breath.

Wondering, *Is it here? Is it yet? Is it now?*

POETRY IS THE SPIRIT OF THE DEAD, WATCHING

I

Unpacking books, shelving them
in the library of this old house,
I come across *The Duel,* a chapbook
Louis Rubin made of poems I wrote
before I left school. The book—
barely worn, inscribed
to the boy who would become
my first husband—just to look at it
makes me touch my face
as if touch might summon back
the girl who, like a distant
relative, faintly
resembles me now.
I turn the pages, perusing
a line here, a line there—
stopped finally
by a title so certain, so absolute,
it takes away my breath.

Poetry Is the Spirit of the Dead, Watching

What on earth did I mean by that?
Who was I reading? Coleridge? Yeats?
The Eliot of *Ash Wednesday*?
Listen. *A moss light
moves the tops of trees,
the hem of a garment walking
in circles; moves patiently and still.* . . .
Easter in the poem,
it was April in western Virginia
beneath Tinker Mountain
where I wrote it, the slim trees
puckering with leaves and early
blossoms, shadblow, flowering judas.

Outside now, a slow rain curtains the house,
sifts through the cedars, beads
on the back of the doe
that crosses the grass in the dark
to eat the day lilies at the garden's
edge. I understand her hunger.
My husband's in bed in another room,
unwell. The fire's made. In Old English
heorth and *heorte,* hearth and heart,
are close.
       Ker, ker—
I imagine the crow's chill call.
Let it center me. *Keramos.*
Cremate. Potter's clay.

The roots of words send out their spirits.

We are measured by our light,
said the hermetic and mild
beloved master of this house,
who raised it from collapse
and ruin. He didn't get
his wish to die here,
where the gate to eternity (he felt)
swung on its hinges
open, shut, open—and is swinging
still, he'd say, as the spirits pass by,
watching.
       Alone tonight,
I'll sit with him, with all the spirits
who made this house, hearth, heart.
I would be *with* them.
       Withed.

II

In the central chimney's great fireplace
the bread oven's set far back—
the woman of the house would have
singed her skirt fetching out the bread,
stirring the kettle of hominy
and winter root crops. In 1680,
a farmer built this house
and scrabbled Connecticut's stones
out of the earth for walls and a pentway,
for the foundation of a carriage house
said to have been made of bird's eye maple.
He kept sheep, farmed what he could
in earth studded with glacial rubble.
The house was built by a *poor* farmer
who set gunstock posts,
rough-hewn beams, chestnut
and oak boards for the walls and floors.
The King's wood, seven
of my hands across, meant for
English ships, he cut and nailed
into the wall behind the cellar door,
unseen. The original family
slept in a smoky loft, collected tolls
from anyone who used the road through
their fields to get to North Stonington,
lived poor, died poor, left the cottage
to descendants who, after a few
generations, moved on.

When Hobart Mitchell found the house
in 1950 poison ivy and trumpet vine
furled out the gape in the slumped roof.
It was a critter's den he bought,
with a hundred acres, and for so little
it makes me know what envy is.

Bought it, patched it, fixed it up
between singing tours and
college semesters, lived here with
one wife who died before him,
and with another, dear Jean,
who died after him six months.
Childless, he left us the house
and the road, having put
the wooded ridges, wetland,
wolf trees, nurse logs, bobcat,
wild turkey, and deer into a land trust.
We have a few of his books—
We Would Not Kill, which he wrote,
also the chapbook of early love poems
he kept in his desk drawer, and
by Gerald Heard, *Prayers and Meditations,*
which he studied and taught before
First Day's Meeting for Worship.
We have his garden tools,
his manuscripts, and a photograph
of the Himalayas steeply white
above a village in Darjeeling. I wear
his college ring, carnelian and gold.
From Jean we have an earthen vase
from Oaxaca, the blue cloth from
Christmas dinners, the china she
chipped when her hands grew clumsy
with arthritis. Because I wanted
to keep their spirits near me,
I purchased from their small estate
a winged thing, a silver maple seed
that could be fastened by a long
sharp pin.
                In this house,
once the designated poor house
in the crossroads town of Preston,
each morning they sat in the silence

of the indwelling Light.
In this room, Hobart used his hands
to heal whoever asked him. At night
for a time they summoned spirits,
moving the planchette across the board,
waiting patiently. They listened to music
before going off to bed and the wild
comfort and wide grace
of their bodies' passion. Outside,
near the well, behind the buckled
old white lilac, Jean
heard a spirit in the wilderness,
so lonely, crying out. She probably
held it in the light—then took it in.

III

How many years ago, sick at heart and tied to the words of a dying argument,
out of my own darkness I offered the Nameless a sudden, single-minded
plea: *show me the center of the self:* and slept hard, dreamless, waking in the dark
with my whole body full of light. And what I saw—though I might now say
wheel or *rose, pulse of fire* or *sunrise*—it was not these. I did not feel joy—I was
it. I blazed. I did not think—*There it is* or *Here.* I blazed. Next moment, I was
touching pillow, collarbone, table, wrist, and thinking in metaphor. Flower
and fruit on a single branch broken off the one body of the world of light.

IV

Tonight, though I would like to ease
the length of my body along the length
of my husband's and enter, breath
by breath, the heat two bodies make,
being *with*—

                tonight I sit by myself
and study the monolith of stone
laid above the fireplace,
imagining the sweat, the struggle,
the sheer will, back-breaking,
and the final pride of heaving
it into place, then the crude clay,
slapped together, to anchor it.
I've seen no lintel stone as great,
but for the one in a crofter's cottage
on Iona—so he was, that Connecticut
farmer, a Scot perhaps, with
bristled eyebrows like my husband's,
like my father's. His, too,
the blue chips of china
I've unearthed in the garden bed
as I shovel down—my muscles sore
with that labor tonight, knees stiff
as I listen to Samuel Barber's
translation of prayer into song—

Thou who art unchangeable,
may we find our rest and remain
in Thee unchanging—

                Kierkegaard's
words, and I see how
one thing builds on another, this room
a poem making room for
Barber, the barred owl's plaintive

hooing in the deep wood,
the far cry of a ferry horn
remembered in the foggy straits
between Mull and Iona—
word on word, stone on
stone, note on note, heaving,
how we rise from the daily midden
of our patch-worked living
and dying.
                    What is prayer
if not a marriage
of passion and the opposing need
for quiet loneliness? What is
a poem, if not the death cry
of each moment's hard-won
and abandoned self? What is
the self?

This house, it's a thin place,
I think. The wind outside
might be the wind that summons
the far-away and brings, as near
as breath, the spirit of the dead
watching.
                    Who *are* you?
I ask the acres of emptiness
into which everything is gathered
and *is*—
turning the question
at last toward my own heart,
blind and stupefied—*Who?*

EAST WINDOW, MOON

It shadows the bed with a lattice of light,
this moon whose ridgepole sinks beneath its own weight,

rising slowly, laboriously, late.

I'm in a new house, unfamiliar to my feet,
strange to fingers that touch the walls uncertainly

as I walk through the dark of it at night.
Outside, different trees, different stones on the path.

Closer to death I want to know great faith *and* great doubt.

What no one taught me, that's what I want to remember,
immersed like Blake, his inner eye

a storehouse for the infinite
flashings the fontanel lets in, before it knits the bone door shut.

I have always been alone, and I have never been alone.

What I used to call *the self* is a windowing of light
in the flood plain of the boundless.

TRYING TO PRAY

The light is such
that now

the beech leaves
anchor

midair gold

against the farther hollows
and afternoon

shadows
beyond the pond

The branches
rise and fall

like swans' wings
soaring

against tether
then, easy

sinking back—

as once, within brief-lit
radiance

someone I
had thought to be

fell impeccably
silent

WHAT IS THE FUNDAMENTAL UNCREATED ESSENCE OF ALL THINGS?

I don't know why
this dried lilac leaf
brings me
near your son's
life—self-fallen,
brief. Too brief.
It resembles the pipal
with its sharp
steeple, as ephemeral
as the sting of
pleasure—remember
the branch lush with flower?
A lure, a snare
not sure enough
to keep us here.
And look, within
the border of the leaf
an empty tree
(given in sparse
calligraphy,
three brushstrokes, four)
and why one might sense
in it *failure*
or *pain* or *grief*
and not a holy silence,
I can't say
having fallen too far
beyond *leaf, self, safe*—
and bowing, not knowing why.

SPOOL OF RED THREAD

As if a surgeon pried inside with a crochet hook, caught up an artery,
    and tugged—

and every tidy thread of blood spilled, spooled itself, coiled round
    and wound into an open

wound I need to staunch . . .

As if, unwinding the spool, I could prepare the needle and take the Chinese red
    silk jacket,

frayed beyond repair, and stitch it up . . .

As if the cirrus web of roads on the map I opened, *sotto voce,* has lifted me
    beyond the city, into an empty red clay field . . .

As if between my legs. A thread of blood, the unraveled smocking of the womb.

STILL LIFE, WITH BINOCULARS

Hot summer night, cicadas . . .
Before I turn off the kitchen light, I pause.

There's a soft breeze: an apparent rustling in the cobalt vase

of dried green hydrangeas, the green Elga uses
in her watercolors for the ripened light of shadows. . . .

And so, on the table below her painting, I've put peaches,
two full plates of them: two plump mangoes,

two bottles of red wine resting on their sides: Merlots:

reflecting in their upturned bases widening halos
of erratic light, through which I look back: years and years:

to bedclothes, rumpled bedclothes
and the wide mirror I'd look into, lying on my side. Who knows

what I longed for then: who knows

what longings from those years I still compose, refuse, or fuse. . . .
Listening now to the cicadas

I see only the doubling of desire long marriage bestows,
and a restless acceptance that grows

beyond desire into ripe stillness: and repose.

IRIS

On its tall stalk, petals deep amethyst
with an under-light of verdigris that flared as the clouds passed
and sun lit its silks,
                        it was a stupa in a forest glade
or the refuge of one who would chant the holy name breath by breath.

It grew in the garden of a woman who had died days before.

I was drawn to it perhaps because of its color,
mysterious as the Old Russian cry to God, *gospodi.*
I did not bow to it.
                        My spine straightened
as I stood quietly there to study its architectural trinities,

petals that opened down as if to touch damp earth, three
that lifted skyward, close enough
to make a tent,
                        a sanctuary
within which three more, lavender and yellow, hovered over

the pistil, white and still. I remembered the door in my old dream,
beyond which, I once thought, the riddle of birth and death
lay revealed.
                        The door was white. It was shining. It was shut—
but no. It wasn't shut. It wasn't even a door. It was the light of a single eye.

Whatever I look at, it looks back.

ON BEING ASKED IF THE ANKLET I'M WEARING IS AN OLD CHARM BRACELET OF MINE

I reply
      by stamping my foot
until the gemstones and pearls are a fierce rush of fire,
a dance called
         taking the shortcut home. . . .

      I reply by pointing to
the cold moon's rim in the whirl and tumble-by river
on whose ripples dove cry scatters. . . .

      I reply with the gesture
the oldest and most purely naked of women would make
to inhabit
         the high wild notes of mountains by the sea. . . .

AIR AND EARTH

As anchor for this lute song, sung in late
midwinter, I hold in mind a ripe pear
from one of the two trees behind your gate,
a dooryard pear, a pear of the back field's
April froth, sun-borne October's firm lute,
if split in half for eating—as you would
split it, eat it, let its pulpy nectar
run down your chin, then spit the seeds out
and whistle.

          That your song, *this* mine—lustral,
and meant to summon you back to the field
I walked, you worked. We'd not have swapped shovels
at the rabbit hole when you lived. I loved
words, their sweet roots. You were of the land,
mud and clay packed tight, and mostly mute—

for all your rough-hewn ways, a gentle man
who liked a flannel shirt, a stogie,
and work out of doors in any weather—more than
anything, liked the truth of hard-to-lie-
still stone walls, the undermining heave of frost,
cedars the cows scratched their backs against,
the fields manured, then mowed: life unadorned,
unaneled—

          you were your own authority.
After you died, on a bright still day, unsure,
I walked the deer-trail, horned-owl, backwoods way
over the stile into your upland pasture.
There I could see. There I could see clear
down to the road that bears your name. If you were
anywhere, I vowed, you'd be here.

I saw a thaw-melt sun, calix gold
on lucent, low patches of ice on the road.
I saw the far lake, blue sky, a tor of clouds
over the bog you cranberried as a child.
I saw what you'd tended, and what left wild
for the red-tailed hawks. *Everett Watson,*
I called, my arms spread wide, wide
as I turned round in the field:

> *you, Everett,*

I know you're out here—and do you know,
the wind swept up the steep field, fierce as a harrow,
but prankish, too, as you had been: a blow,
a sough, a rough kiss, a rollicking volute,
a whet of appetite. Was it your Spirit?
Wind, for sure. But evidence of spirit,

particular spirit—yours—there was none.
The wind was traceless. If an expanse of spirit,
also a tumult I had to own.
I wanted you come back to ease my heart.
Why must you die—why must I?
The big wind had no answer. The wind
had no answer. It was your quiet,
magnified. It was nothing I could know.
Even so,

> I say *lute, light, pear tree, gate.*

Now, I say it. Song is its own authority.
Then, I stood in the quiet of your field.
Wiregrass bent its whole length along the earth,
a flare of light unfolding—and the light
and garlands of wind, spread low, were enough.

TRANSPARENT

One day I will not wake in my body as you know it,
or go from the bed to the open
door to breathe in the fresh glory of the morning.

Although you will not see me, by afternoon I will be
wind, unfenced in the expanse
between towering clouds of oyster and plum air.

I will be in the oak, in the ivy, in the spillway
and banks thick with iris,
yellow-eyed and blue, and in the tannic and bittersweet

silk of the pond over which clouds pause and reflect
before shattering the surface.
I will be in the rain, in the stone, in the root, in the fruits

of the garden. You will take me into your mouth
(as so often you have)
and we will be one body of solitudes and barrens and wilds.

We will be mountain and cirrus, salamander, owl in the dark
husk of winter, a crescendo
of cicadas in summer. We will fly in a green flash of light

over fields taking shape in the early morning mists. Here,
always here. So close, there is
nothing deeper I can tell you than what we already know.

NOTES

Part I is dedicated to the memory of Jean North Mitchell.

The title "What Cannot Be Kissed Away" is from a phrase of Jane Hirshfield's.
"All the way to heaven is heaven" is from Catherine of Siena ("Ashes").
Charles Chu is a painter and calligrapher who lives in New London, Connecticut.

Part II

I wish to thank James Scully for his thoughtful suggestions as "Fuel," "Moment,"
    and "Respect" evolved.
"Respect" is dedicated to Richiena Brown.
"One Body" is dedicated to Peter Matthiessen.

Part III is dedicated to the memory of my father, mother, and sister.

"Word over all, beautiful as the sky" is from Walt Whitman ("Elegy for My Father").
"Ask Me Now" is for my sister Elizabeth.

Part IV is dedicated to the memory of Hobart Mitchell.

"blind and stupefied" is from William Butler Yeats ("Poetry Is the Spirit of the
    Dead, Watching").
"What is the Fundamental Uncreated Essence of All Things?" is for Lysbet Rogers.
"Iris" is dedicated to Marcia Kelly and Francoise Krampf.
"On Being Asked . . ." is for Sam Pickering, who asked the question.
"the high wild notes of mountains by the sea" is from Gary Snyder.

"Transparent" is for David and our life of waking up together.